ID0908859

A LOOK AT ANCIENT CIVILIZATIONS

ANCIENT CHINA

BY DANIEL R. FAUST

Gareth Stevens
PUBLISHING

CRASHCOURSE

Please visit our website, www.garethstevens.com. For a free color catalog of all our high-quality books, call toll free 1-800-542-2595 or fax 1-877-542-2596.

Cataloging-in-Publication Data

Names: Faust, Daniel R.
Title: Ancient China / Daniel R. Faust.
Description: New York : Gareth Stevens Publishing, 2019. | Series: A look at ancient civilizations | Includes glossary and index.
Identifiers: LCCN ISBN 9781538231463 (pbk.) | ISBN 9781538230046 (library bound) | ISBN 9781538233221 (6 pack)
Subjects: LCSH: China--Civilization--To 221 B.C.--Juvenile literature. | China--Civilization--221 B.C.-960 A.D.--Juvenile literature.
Classification: LCC DS741.65 F385 2019 | DDC 931--dc23

First Edition

Published in 2019 by
Gareth Stevens Publishing
111 East 14th Street, Suite 349
New York, NY 10003

Designer: Reann Nye
Editor: Tayler Cole

Photo credits: Series art (writing background) mcherevan/Shutterstock.com, (map) Andrey_Kuzmin/Shutterstock.com; cover, p. 1 aphotostory/Shutterstock.com; p. 5 simpletun/Shutterstock.com; p. 7 Vixit/Shutterstock.com; p. 9 ekler/Shutterstock.com; p. 11 (top) Chatrawee Wiratgasem/Shutterstock.com; p. 11 (bottom) beboy/Shutterstock.com; p. 13 Purplexsu/Shutterstock.com; p. 15 Ismoon/Editor at Large/Wikipedia.org; p. 17 Carlos Amarillo/Shutterstock.com; p. 19 360b/Shutterstock.com; p. 21 TonyV3112/Shutterstock.com; p. 23 beibaoke/Shutterstock.com; p. 25 Erena.Wilson/Shutterstock.com; p. 27 aminphotoz/Shutterstock.com; p. 29 Siegfried Layda/Photographer's Choice/Getty Images.

Printed in the United States of America

CPSIA compliance information: Batch #CW19GS: For further information contact Gareth Stevens, New York, New York at 1-800-542-2595.

CONTENTS

Words in the glossary appear in **bold** type the first time they are used in the text.

THE WORLD'S OLDEST CIVILIZATION

China is unlike other ancient civilizations. Most ancient civilizations were conquered, or taken over, by outsiders. Their cultures, or ways of life, were often lost. Even though China would also be conquered by outsiders, these groups changed very little about Chinese culture.

Make The Grade

The culture of ancient China is almost the same as the culture of modern-day China. This is why China is said to be the oldest continuous civilization in the world.

MOUNTAINS AND DESERTS

For most of its history, China has been **isolated** because of its mountains and deserts. These large, dangerous landforms made it hard for outsiders to invade, or enter, China. The deserts to the west and north of China are some of the largest in the world!

Make The Grade

Along the southern border of China are the Himalayas,
which have some of the tallest mountains in the world!

THE YELLOW RIVER

The Yellow River, or Huang He, of northern China is the second longest river in the country. It's also known as the **cradle** of Chinese civilization. Thousands of years ago, ancient people started settling along the Yellow River, building villages and farms.

8

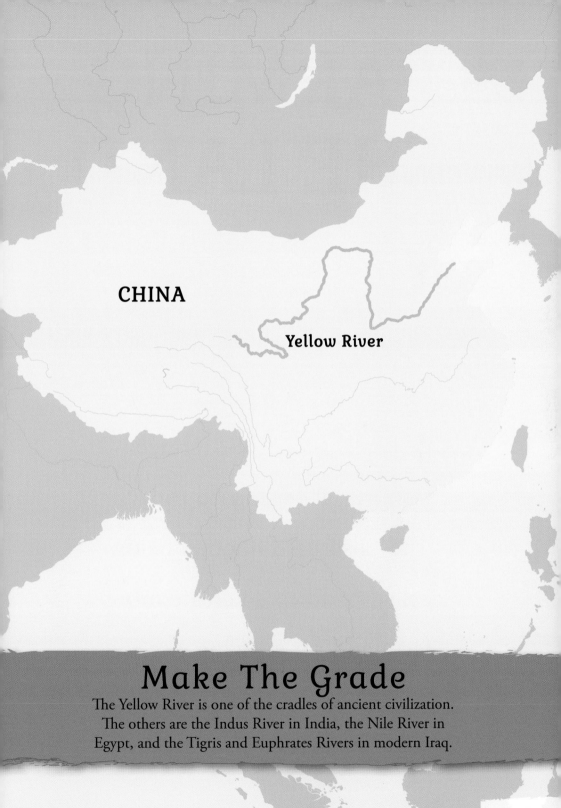

CHINA

Yellow River

Make The Grade

The Yellow River is one of the cradles of ancient civilization.
The others are the Indus River in India, the Nile River in
Egypt, and the Tigris and Euphrates Rivers in modern Iraq.

FARMING THE LAND

China doesn't have much good farmland. Ancient Chinese farmers cut into the sides of mountains in order to grow crops. This is called terrace farming. It's still used today. They also used flooded fields, called paddies, to create more farmland for growing rice.

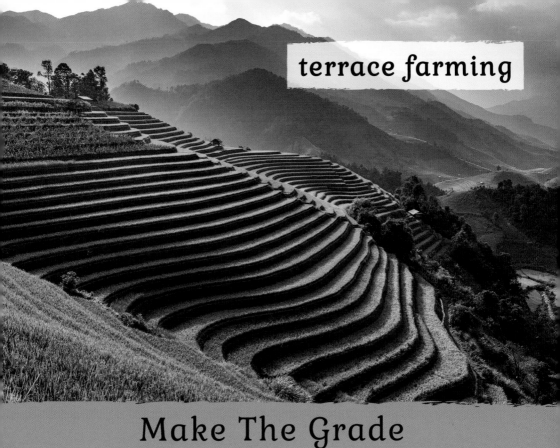

terrace farming

Make The Grade

The earliest crops grown in China were rice and millet,
a kind of grain. Farmers had to grow a lot of food
to feed all the people in China.

rice paddy

THE RISE OF DYNASTIES

Until the early 1900s, China was ruled by dynasties. A dynasty is a line of rulers who belong to a single family. Some ruling families believed in the mandate, or official order, of heaven. This was the idea that heaven gave an **emperor** the right to rule.

Make The Grade

Some people think the Xia dynasty was the first to rule China.
Legend says the dynasty was founded by Yu, a man who saved
China by getting rid of the water left by a great flood.

13

The first dynasty to leave behind **artifacts** was the Shang dynasty, which ruled from about 1600 BC to 1046 BC. The people of the Shang dynasty had an advanced culture. They used a metal called bronze to make weapons, tools, and religious items.

Make The Grade

More than 100,000 bones and shells have been found
from the Shang dynasty. These religious artifacts have the
earliest known form of Chinese writing on them.

After the Shang dynasty
came the Zhou dynasty,
which lasted from 1046 BC
to 256 BC. During this time,
people started using iron to
make tools and weapons.
Farming became easier and
the number of people in
China grew.

Make The Grade

The Zhou dynasty lasted longer than any other dynasty
in Chinese history. Many important people lived
during this time, including Confucius!

THE FIRST EMPIRE

The Qin dynasty began in 221 BC and **united** China for the first time. *Qin* which sounds like "chin," is believed to be where the modern name "China" comes from. The first emperor connected walls built around the empire. These walls were ancient parts of what's now called the Great Wall of China.

Make The Grade

When the Qin dynasty ended, the Han dynasty rose to
power. The Han dynasty was a **golden age** in Chinese
history, with great advances made in art and science.

19

CONFUCIANISM AND DAOISM

China is the birthplace of Confucianism and Taoism. These two **philosophies** created the Chinese culture that's still around today. Confucianism teaches the importance of **responsibility** and kindness. Taoism teaches its followers to live a simple and **moral** life.

Make The Grade

Buddhism may have come to China from India as early as 300 BC.
Buddhism, Confucianism, and Taoism are called the "three teachings"
because they're the most important philosophies in Chinese culture.

THE MONGOLS INVADE

In the early 1200s, China was taken over by the **Mongols**. However, Chinese culture changed very little. When the Mongolian leader Kublai Khan ruled, he took on the role of Chinese emperor and even created a new dynasty called the Yuan dynasty.

Make The Grade

The Mongols created a huge empire that connected Asian and Middle Eastern civilizations. This led to the spread of ideas and goods between China and western countries.

SILK, SPICES, AND PORCELAIN

Beginning around 2,000 years ago, goods and ideas began being traded along the Silk Road. The Silk Road was a trade route that ran between modern-day Europe and China. The Chinese sold items such as paper, spices, and tea. In return, they bought wool, gold, and glass.

Make The Grade

Silk was valuable in China. At first, it was only worn by the emperor and upper classes. Silk showed everyone else how important they were.

China had many special items to trade. Spices, teas, and sugar were highly valued. Many people in western countries also wanted Chinese porcelain and gunpowder. Languages and ideas about science, philosophy, and religion were also shared along the Silk Road.

Make The Grade

Many items that are common today were invented in ancient China. The Chinese had invented paper by AD 105, and they were printing books hundreds of years before Europeans!

porcelain

27

ARMY FOR THE DEAD

Historians are still learning about ancient China. In 1974, an underground room full of about 8,000 terra-cotta, or clay, soldiers was discovered. Scientists think this army was buried with China's first Qin emperor to join him after death.

Make The Grade

The soldiers all have different faces, armor, and weapons.
There are even **chariots** being pulled by clay horses!

29

TIMELINE OF ANCIENT CHINA

c. 1600–1046 BC
The Shang dynasty rules.

1046–256 BC
The Zhou dynasty rules.

c. 550 BC
Confucianism begins
to spread.

c. 300 BC
Buddhism may have first
appeared in China.

221 BC
The Qin dynasty comes to
power and unites China.

206 BC–AD 220
The Han dynasty rules and
China enters a golden age.

1200s
The Mongols take over
China and set up the
Yuan dynasty.

GLOSSARY

artifact: something made by humans in the past

chariot: a two-wheeled wagon that was pulled by horses

cradle: the place where something begins

emperor: the ruler of an empire. An empire is a large area of land under the control of a single ruler.

golden age: a time of great happiness, success, and achievement

isolate: to keep apart from others

legend: a story that has been passed down for many, many years that is unlikely to be true

Mongols: a group of people from a region of central Asia that is today the country of Mongolia and part of northern China

moral: based on what you think is right and good

philosophy: a system of thought made to try to understand the nature of that which is real

responsibility: a duty or task you are required or expected to do

unite: to cause two or more things to join together and become one thing

FOR MORE INFORMATION

BOOKS

Herron, Pamela. *Exploring Ancient China*. Mankato, MN: 12-Story Library, 2018.

Randolph, Joanne. *Living and Working in Ancient China*. New York, NY: Enslow Publishing, 2018.

WEBSITE

Ancient China

www.dkfindout.com/us/history/ancient-china/

Explore this website to find out more about the terra-cotta soldiers, Chinese writing, and Confucius.

Publisher's note to educators and parents: Our editors have carefully reviewed this website to ensure that it is suitable for students. Many websites change frequently, however, and we cannot guarantee that a site's future contents will continue to meet our high standards of quality and educational value. Be advised that students should be closely supervised whenever they access the internet.

INDEX